You Know You're an
EMPTY NESTER
When...

YOU KNOW YOU'RE AN EMPTY NESTER WHEN...
A HILARIOUS LOOK AT LIFE AFTER KIDS

DIANNE SUNDBY, Ph.D.

Illustrations by Jeff Law

SPECIALIST PRESS INTERNATIONAL

New York

For further information, contact:

99 Spring Street, 3rd Floor
New York, NY 10012
Tel: (212) 431-5011
Fax: (212) 431-8646
E-mail: *publicity@spibooks.com*
Visit us at *www.spibooks.com*

10 9 8 7 6 5 4 3 2 1
First Edition

Library of Congress Cataloging-in-Publication Data available.
ISBN: 1-56171-885-8

For My Family

Mike, Jenn, Steve, and Maia
You're the best!

Acknowledgments

Several people contributed to the completion of this book.
Many thanks to my publisher, Ian Shapolsky, and the staff at Specialist
Press International in New York, my editor, Cliff Carle, my illustrator,
Jeff Law, and my page designer, David Aaron. Without all of their helpful
suggestions, I'd still be on page one.

Special thanks to the empty-nest parents I've had the privilege to know
through my practice—and for being there for my own "life after kids"
times, the Marlborough Moms—a potluck dinner group who've contin-
ued to get together since our daughters packed up for college. The
camaraderie and sharing of life without our kids certainly helped me in
my adjustment to being an empty nester—and in putting together this
book.

And, lots of thanks to Marcia Shourt, Christine Patrick, June Bilgore,
Juliette and Kevin Scanlon, and Shelley Stamm for their helpful com-
ments, and especially Mike Driver, my husband and co-empty nester,
who patiently read my "words in progress"—and even laughed!

The Driver kids—Jenn, Steve, and Maia—what would my life be
without you! Thanks for being you! I love you lots!

Introduction

YOU KNOW YOU'RE AN EMPTY NESTER WHEN...is a product of my personal experience. When our youngest child left for college, my life took a dramatic shift—like going from *drive* to *park* at 100 m.p.h.— a screeching halt to the familiar life I had learned to navigate: life with "a kid at home."

While I had always worked as a psychologist, I also spent a large chunk of my time going to my kids' school events, games, plays, and concerts—and had dished out years of holiday pizza lunches on room-mom duty. Before my kids could drive, I took my turn with carpools for AYSO soccer and Little League practices, karate, and ballet lessons—plus, I shuttled my kids to scouts, music rehearsals, and tennis meets—and *always* on time—well, *mostly* always.

With my youngest child suddenly 3,000 miles away at college, I now had what seemed like an unnerving amount of free time. How to fill it was the perplexing question. Rock climbing, sky diving, and bungee jumping were certainly options—yeah right! Actually, it was the process of venturing into this "off-road terrain" of life-after-kids that led to this book.

In the course of that first empty-nest year, it occurred to me that we moms spend nine months before birth incubating our kids—then well over nine months adjusting to their leaving the nest. That time, post-kids' leaving the nest, is a topic I thought might be helpful for both moms and dads to read and reflect on—and, hopefully, have a few laughs at the same time.

It is my hope that this book will help all of you new, as well as up-and-coming empty nesters, facilitate your transition from the "known world" as a parent of kids at home to the "unknown world" of being an empty nester. And, for you veterans, may this be a pleasant re-visit of memories from that "post-kids" time.

I firmly believe—and there's a ton of research to support this idea— that if we can chuckle at ourselves and our frustrations as we experience new phases in life, we will not only better survive the changes, but actually enjoy ourselves along the way.

Introducing...

Stacy

Norm

Honey

Debbie

Dave

Jake

An Additional Note

As I considered cartoons to illustrate the craziness of "life after kids," I found myself drawn to the idea of presenting two sets of empty-nest parents, one with a daughter, and one with a son. As I thought about these parents' empty-nest experiences, the characters began to take on a life of their own. And, since I felt I knew them, I gave them first names. Please enjoy Jeff Law's illustrations of "Empty-Nest Life" as experienced by *Norm* and *Honey*, parents of *Stacy*, and *Debbie* and *Dave*, parents of *Jake*.

And, on behalf of my publisher, SPI Books, I would like to call your attention to the last page of this book concerning a future edition and YOUR personal empty-nest experiences. We would love to hear from you!

Now, on to *You Know You're an Empty Nester When…*

Sincerely,

Dr. Dianne Sundby

You pay for a week's worth of groceries with a $20.00 bill—and actually get change back!

You Know You're an EMPTY NESTER When...

You buy so many boxes of
"Just Thinking About You" greeting cards,
that Hallmark's stock jumps ten points.

You finally get around to completing
your kid's baby book.

You Know You're an EMPTY NESTER When...

You go for a long drive and actually miss hearing, "Are we there yet?"

During a phone conversation, your daughter sneezes. The next day she opens an overnight package from you and finds: Vitamin C, Kleenex, Chapstick, Robitussin, Cough Drops, and a case of chicken soup.

You have a party and no one calls the cops.

You Know You're an EMPTY NESTER When...

Your hotel room for your kid's college graduation is reserved—two weeks into her freshman year.

Your cat looks at you quizzically,
and your first response is, "Because I said so!"

You Know You're an EMPTY NESTER When...

Now that your daughter's daily two-hour showers
are a thing of the past, your neighborhood is
no longer on water rationing.

The post office express-mail clerk knows
your kid's address by heart.

You phone other "empty nesters" to commiserate—
no matter that their kids left home thirty years ago.

You Know You're an
EMPTY NESTER
When...

You wonder why the house is now so quiet—
Oh yeah, your kid's stereo system went with him!

To make sure no one drops by to interrupt you the
night your kid's scheduled to call home, you nail a
"Quarantine" sign on your door.

You Know You're an
EMPTY NESTER
When...

Hoping to get letters from your kid, you send self-addressed, stamped envelopes off with him.

When they are not used, you send self-addressed, stamped postcards with one box to check—
☐ I AM STILL ALIVE!

The phone rings and it's for you.

You Know You're an EMPTY NESTER When...

You try to stay connected to your kid in his absence by listening to his favorite rock group—30 seconds into what he calls "music," you suddenly remember you really should call that nice telemarketer back.

You Know You're an **EMPTY NESTER** *When...*

UNREAD

CAREERS

READ

You have time to read every section of the Sunday newspaper—including the Career Classifieds— and you're not even looking for a job.

You Know You're an
EMPTY NESTER
When...

Now that your sports savvy son has moved out,
your "Sports IQ" is lower than
Shaq's free-throw percentage.

Blissfully, you bake up a batch of cookies for your
kid's care package—then curse all the way home
from the post office—how were you to know your
package would exceed their weight limit?

You Know You're an
EMPTY NESTER
When...

Your main extra-curricular activity is wondering
what to do now that your kid no longer
has extra-curricular activities.

Even your junk mail gets opened!

After years and years of putting it off, you finally get around to cleaning out your garage, and now your dining room table has a proud new centerpiece: your kid's 3rd Grade Mud Creatures Science Project.

You subscribe to at least five daily newspapers—
just for the crossword puzzles.

With your kid's school athletic events a thing
of the past, the only drama in your life is on
Jerry Springer and *Oprah*.

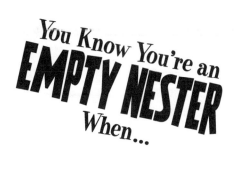

You see a pile of wet towels on your bathroom floor
and are overcome by a wave of nostalgia.

You Know You're an EMPTY NESTER When...

You consider working out for the first time since your last "Mommy and Me" Gymboree Class.

Thoughts of the above bring to mind the wise adage, "If it ain't broke, don't fix it."

You Know You're an EMPTY NESTER When...

You clean out your kid's closet, make the thrift shop rounds with carloads of out-dated surfer shirts, Moonboots, and Pac-Man games—and find yourself flashing $50.00 bills just to get someone to take these things off your hands.

You Know You're an EMPTY NESTER When...

You've invited your long-lost relatives to visit,
then cousins twice-removed—now you're about
ready to pick random names out of the phonebook...

...Two weeks later...

You Know You're an EMPTY NESTER When...

Salsa Dancing replaces attending your kid's Back-to-School Night.

You realize you actually miss the high school principal's phone calls—the ones checking up on your kid's whereabouts.

As you renew your movie rental card, you wonder
why there aren't frequent *viewer* miles.

You Know You're an EMPTY NESTER When...

You arrange business trips to places that are
near your kid—basically anywhere
outside the Arctic Circle.

You Know You're an
EMPTY NESTER
When...

You look forward to spending quality time
with your goldfish.

You Know You're an EMPTY NESTER When...

You can now stock up on all the food your kid whined about: Brussels sprouts, beets, sardines, liverwurst, lutefisk…

You Know You're an
EMPTY NESTER
When...

You now have your car again—along with
five Hip Hop CDs, a half-slurped Slurpee,
and ten petrified McNuggets.

You Know You're an EMPTY NESTER When...

You schedule your grocery shopping
around talk radio.

Your dog has better manicured nails than you.

You go out to a week-night theatre performance
for the first time in decades. At intermission,
you rush out to call home, forgetting that
your dog doesn't pick up the phone.

You Know You're an
EMPTY NESTER
When...

Noting the absence of activity at your address,
your pizza delivery guy calls to ask if you're okay.

You dig out the old cookbooks you adored—and use them as cooling trays for microwaved dinners.

You can't quite let go of the urge to help with your kid's Halloween costume—only now, the question is, "Should your dog go as the young Elvis, or the middle-aged Elvis?"

You almost got killed taking down
the basketball hoop...

...then put it back up the minute your kid says he'll be home for the weekend.

You Know You're an
EMPTY NESTER
When...

You throw away the lock to the liquor cabinet...

…then rush out to buy a new one—
just minutes before your kid arrives home.

You Know You're an EMPTY NESTER When...

Where you once got *squinty-eyed* proof-reading
your kid's college applications,
now you squint over AARP publications' fine print.

Your freezer, which used to bulge with frozen pizza and fudgesicles, now bulges with "Lite 'n Lean" microwave dinners.

You Know You're an EMPTY NESTER When...

Your December holiday shopping is
completed by Labor Day.

Your "Thank You" notes are written
before your gifts arrive.

Hearing "You've Got Mail" is akin to
winning the lottery—no matter
it's your twenty-fifth spam that day.

You Know You're an EMPTY NESTER When...

Labor Day, usually spent battling crowds
to buy your kid's back-to-school stuff,
now is actually a day of no labor.

You apply for every pre-approved credit card
just to get the introductory offer:
free airline miles!

You Know You're an EMPTY NESTER When...

You stay up later and sleep in still later and know much more about Conan O'Brien than Katie Couric.

You no longer call in sick at work so you can attend your kid's afternoon soccer game—now you call in sick because you're sick.

You Know You're an EMPTY NESTER When...

You look back at all the times you wished
you could have more time to yourself,
and compare it to the day you just spent—
then curse the Wish Fairy for going overboard.

You Know You're an EMPTY NESTER When...

You've finally had to clear the refrigerator door of your kid's grade school Honor Certificates to make room for Early-Bird Dinner Coupons.

You Know You're an EMPTY NESTER When...

You spend so much time with web chain letters and
surfing the internet
that your virus software uninstalls itself!

You Know You're an EMPTY NESTER When...

More than once, you've had to explain to
a passer-by why you were talking to yourself.

You Know You're an
EMPTY NESTER
When...

You're more up-to-date on current events than
Dan Rather and Peter Jennings combined.

You join Book-of-the-Month clubs
and actually read their books.

You Know You're an
EMPTY NESTER
When...

You think about visiting your kid unannounced...

...then remember how that went over in your day!

You Know You're an
EMPTY NESTER
When...

Seminars on raising your hormone levels
replace seminars on raising your kid's SATs.

You consider getting back into your
"pre-kid" bicycling activity—until you
remember how form-fitting those biking pants are.

You Know You're an
EMPTY NESTER
When...

Your husband ponders the point of your
gourmet cooking class, as night after night
it's the usual burgers and fries.

You Know You're an EMPTY NESTER When...

You actually miss writing excuses for your kid's late English papers—you were getting pretty good with variations on Flu 101.

You seek out jury duty.

You Know You're an
EMPTY NESTER
When...

You pick out some on-sale clothes for yourself,
then put them on hold. You just remembered
your phone bill—due tomorrow—
has quadrupled since your kid moved out.

You Know You're an EMPTY NESTER When...

Pregnancy abdominal stretch marks were once a main topic of conversation with your girlfriends—now, you look at each other's faces and ask, "Did my doctor Botox too much?!"

Your kid comes home and your cat looks offended.

You Know You're an EMPTY NESTER When...

You thought cooking for your daughter in high school was impossible when she turned Vegetarian—now she's a Vegan!

After your kid's first vacation stay with you, you request that she call when she gets back to her dorm. Your heart sinks when you hear the words, "Hi, I'm Home!"

On the plus side, you no longer have to feign an interest in MTV.

You Know You're an
EMPTY NESTER
When...

Your kid likes to joke that your
school yearbook was recently discovered
in an archeological dig.

At least once a day you walk into a room
and forget why you're there.

Your kitchen re-model project gets postponed
indefinitely over the worry that your kid
will head for the refrigerator and
find himself opening the oven instead.

You Know You're an EMPTY NESTER When...

You find yourself hunting down and hugging
your kid's mangy teddy bear—
the one you tried for years to dump.

You Know You're an EMPTY NESTER When...

You sign up for a Nutrition class,
then immediately drop out when you learn
you'll have to surrender your Krispy Kremes.

You Know You're an
EMPTY NESTER
When...

You can't resist getting more frequent flyer mileage points—even though it's your fifth phone company switch of the month.

Panic sets in—finally a letter from your kid—
and you can't find your reading glasses.

You no longer worry about losing your reading
glasses—you've put a pair in every room.

You show up for your yearly mammogram
and sadly realize this is the only time
someone will want you to appear topless.

You Know You're an **EMPTY NESTER** *When...*

You no longer get to use your kid's
extra-curriculars to get out of social obligations.
Now you have to come up with your *own* excuses.

Your college kid's favorite book is your check book.

Phone conversations with your kid are
short because of time schedules—
your kid's, of course, not yours.

You Know You're an EMPTY NESTER When...

You merrily browse through the
Junior Department tank tops, looking for a gift—
until a pint-sized sales girl suggests
you might find what you're looking for
in the plus-sizes.

You decide you're ready to try out one of
the new electronic devices your kid raves about—
you scan the set-up guide—and immediately have to
call your kid to walk you through the directions.

You Know You're an EMPTY NESTER When...

You wait impatiently for your kid to come home for winter break—then she immediately goes on vacation with her friends.

You know that you should always plan extra
time before going out—it's a given you
won't remember where you put your car keys.

Reality hits hard as you finally pack up
your maternity clothes for Good Will.

You Know You're an EMPTY NESTER When...

"Waist Watchers" hangs up when you call about weighing your dog's gourmet kibbles.

You Know You're an
EMPTY NESTER
When...

You spend so much on pet toys and
gourmet kibbles that you could
support an expedition to Mars.

You get a canine pal for your dog,
and are now spending enough to bring
the Mars expedition back.

You eye the 2-door sports cars on the road—
then realize that two 70-pound dogs in the
passenger seat might be a bit too cozy.

You Know You're an EMPTY NESTER When...

Those stiff finger joints make it tough to open your childproof anti-arthritis pill containers.

You don't worry any more about answering
the phone in the buff.

You decide to "Feng Shui" your house,
but are told you'll have to put a
Great Wall around your kid's room.

Some of Martha Stewart's ideas actually
start to seem practical.

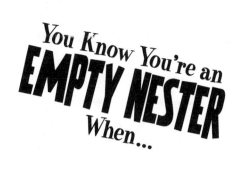

You still can't believe that at-home romantic interludes no longer have to be behind closed doors.

Your dog gets increasingly spoiled...

...after the 4th walk of the day...

...he decides to pretend he's asleep.

Your favorite tee reads,
"I sent my kid to Europe, and all he
got me was this lousy T-shirt."

You Know You're an EMPTY NESTER When...

Your huge dental bills are no longer for your kid's braces—they're for your partials.

You realize your dentist is the same age as your kid.

You take great pride in your
A to Z medicine cabinet
alphabetization accomplishment.

You Know You're an EMPTY NESTER When...

As you sit in the passenger seat of your car
at a red light, you realize you've gone
from begging your kid to drive slower
to begging your spouse to drive faster.

You Know You're an EMPTY NESTER When...

You really look forward to
the downhill part of hikes.

You start to worry about your hearing when your kid asks *you* to turn the radio down.

You take a nostalgic drive past your kid's
Little League park and discover that
his teammates are now the coaches.

Your kid's driving record
is now better than yours.

You Know You're an EMPTY NESTER When...

You wish *all* slacks came...

POP

...with elastic waistbands.

You Know You're an EMPTY NESTER When...

You debate whether to pay full price
for your movie ticket...

MOVIE TICKETS

P R I C E S

ADULT..............$9.00

SENIOR
   55 & OVER.......$6.00

CHILD.............$6.00

…or admit to being a senior citizen.

Alarm bells go off when you realize
that whenever a child is born—
so is a grandmother.

You guess it's probably time to replace
those desk-top baby pictures
with your kid's wedding portraits.

You're getting wedding invitations
from the kids your kid used to baby-sit.

You debate converting your kid's room
into a guest room—
After all, she *only* moved out
twenty years ago.

You Know You're an EMPTY NESTER When...

Your shoe heels are at least...

...4 inches shorter than your daughter's.

You Know You're an
EMPTY NESTER
When...

Depression sets in when you open
a 25th High School Reunion invitation—
and discover it's for your kid.

It seems there's more silver in your hair
than in your silverware drawer.

Those skinny, little candles on your cake
have been permanently replaced
by one, big fat candle.

Your daughter's prom dress
is featured in a vintage shop window.

You Know You're an EMPTY NESTER When...

Your heart stops for a second when your kid
actually asks you for career advice.

Your kid orders the wine at dinner.

You Know You're an EMPTY NESTER When...

After all is said and done, you *finally*
understand that when
the "nesting door" closes...

YOU DON'T KNOW WHAT FUN IS!

SLAM!

...another one opens—
and it's not being slammed
by a shrieking teenager!

About the Author

Dr. Dianne Sundby is a licensed psychologist whose private practice addresses both therapeutic and career change concerns. Upon receiving her doctorate from Purdue University, she lectured at the University of Southern California for several years, directed clinical service programs, and supervised a number of psychological research projects. Her writings include papers and book chapters on dual-career families and the personality dynamics associated with specific careers. In addition to psychotherapy, counseling, assessment, and research work, she has consulted extensively in the United States and abroad on issues concerning management and employee selection and development. She is a founding partner of DS Consulting (DSC), a firm that addresses a wide variety of organizational issues, including career development. In addition, Dr. Sundby is the co-author of a creativity assessment procedure and a career preference inventory, and is currently developing a decision-making exercise to determine how an individual thinks in an ambiguous social situation.

A member of the American Psychological Association, Dr. Sundby has appeared as a guest psychologist on several television and radio programs and is interviewed and quoted frequently by a number of national, as well as Los Angeles-based publications.

She is involved with several philanthropic groups and currently serves as advisor to the Coronets, a young women's social service group, affiliated with the Los Angeles Chapter of the National Charity League. Dr. Sundby, the empty-nest mother of three, lives in Los Angeles with her husband, Mike, and their two dogs, Kobi and Taigar.

Attention Readers

Specialist Press International welcomes you to submit YOUR
personal empty-nest experiences for inclusion in our forthcoming
More—You Know You're an Empty Nester When...
We will, with your permission, list the names of those whose
experiences were selected on a page designated for contributors.
In addition, you will receive a complimentary copy
of the *Empty Nester (II)* book.

Please E-mail to: Emptynesting2@aol.com

OR

Mail to: Empty Nesting II Submissions
c/o DSC
9229 W. Sunset Boulevard, Suite 502
Los Angeles, CA 90069

Thanks. We look forward to hearing from you!

MORE ART OF CLOSING ANY DEAL • James Pickens

This book offers clever, gutsy and even slightly devious techniques that will bring you success at the closing table. You learn: the right and wrong times for managers to step in and help salesmen with customers; dozens of sure-fire techniques, deadly traps and imaginative ruses that sales closers and managers can coordinate; what all sales closers must know about managers–and vice versa.

Retail Price: $18.95 • Special Price: $15.95

Hard • 6" x 9" • 276 pgs • ISBN: 0-944007-58-9

HUNT/KILL SELLING: *Sales Secrets Of The Professional Persuaders* by Jack Matthews

This is a valuable tool for everyone involved in selling. 40 yrs. of sales secrets by America's top sales traner are revealed here.

If you want increased salesmanship from your sales team or from yourself, this is the ultimate book you must read!

Retail Price: $19.95 • Special Price: $12.95

Hard • 6" x 9" • 264 pgs • ISBN: 0-944007-78-3

AVOIDING THE PITFALLS OF STARTING YOUR OWN BUSINESS by Jeferey Davidson

Nine out of ten new businesses don't last long enough to become old ones. Too many entrepreneurs make highly avoidable errors–and then lose their life savings, their friends, marriages, and their self-respect. Whether you are contemplating a new business or you want to know more about today's scene, you need the no-nonsense advice of a Certified Management Consultant like Davidson. From his extensive files of actual case experiences he shares wise insights for aspiring entrepreneurs.

Retail Price: $10.95 • Special Price: $9.95

Trade • 6" x 9" • 260 pgs • ISBN: 1-56171-011-3

POWER AND PROTOCOL FOR GETTING TO THE TOP: *The Image, The Moves, The Smarts For Business And Social Success*
by Jeffrey Davidson

Ability & advanced degrees aren't enough to get you to the top–you have to talk, walk, dress & think like the power people who are in charge. You'll learn all the techniques to develop your own personal image of power.

Retail Price: $19.95 • Special Price: $14.95

Hard • 6" x 9" • 246 pgs • ISBN: 0-944007-68-6

TRUE CRIME/CONSPIRACY TITLES FROM S.P.I. BOOKS!

DISHONORED GAMES: *Corruption, Money & Greed At The Olympics*
by Vyv Simson & Andrew Jennings

Every four years, the Olympics are celebrated with a flood of congratulatory coverage. In all the books, articles and documentaries extolling the beauty and purity of the Olympic Ideal, only cursory notice is given to the Lausanne-based International Olympic Committee (I.O.C.) and its secretive management. These British journalists/authors explode the carefully cultivated image and idealistic hype behind the I.O.C. and its self-perpetuating leadership.

Retail Price: $19.95 • Special Price: $14.95

Hard • 6" x 9" • 320 pgs • ISBN: 1-56171-199-3

COMPROMISED: *Clinton, Bush and The CIA*
by Terry Reed & John Cummings

Reed, A CIA asset turned into a fugitive for opposing government drug trafficking, presents damning evidence placing Bill Clinton and George Bush (Senior) directly in the Iran-Contra loop, complete with a trail of Contra training, money laundering, dealings with Oliver North, the involvement of the U.S. Attorney General, and much more. Damning to both political parties.

Retail Price: $23.95 • Special Price: $18.00

Hard • 6" x 9" • 496 pgs • ISBN: 1-56171-249-3

ENTERTAINMENT TITLES FROM S.P.I. BOOKS!

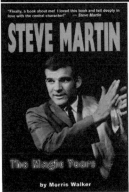

"Finally, a book about me! I loved this book and fell deeply in love with the central character!" — *Steve Martin*

STEVE MARTIN: *The Magic Years*
by Morris Walker

A "must-buy, must-read" for the millions of fans who have been kept in the dark by the secretive superstar, who claims he'll never write an autobiography. This is the closest thing to an autobiography...Written by Steve's best friend... and it's even endorsed by Steve Martin! The book is packed with never-before-told vignettes and humorous true stories that forged Steve's unmistakable, charismatic presence.

by Morris Walker

Retail Price: $22.95 • Special Price: $18.00

Hard • 6" x 9" • 50 B&W photos • 320 pgs • ISBN: 1-56171-980-3